SCIENCE Q&A

TRANSPORTATION TECHNOLOGY

 Cavendish Square

New York

Published in 2016 by Cavendish Square Publishing, LLC
243 5th Avenue, Suite 136, New York, NY 10016

© 2016 Brown Bear Books Ltd

First Edition

Website: cavendishsq.com

CPSIA Compliance Information: Batch #WS15CSQ

Library of Congress Cataloging-in-Publication Data

Transportation technology / edited by Tim Harris.
p. cm. — (Science Q&A)
Includes index.
ISBN 978-1-50260-628-0 (hardcover) ISBN 978-1-50260-627-3 (paperback)
ISBN 978-1-50260-629-7 (ebook)
1. Transportation engineering — Juvenile literature. 2. Motor vehicles — Juvenile literature. 3. Transportation — Juvenile literature. I. Harris, Tim.
II. Title.

TA1149.H37 2015
629.04—d23

For Brown Bear Books Ltd:
Editors: Tracey Kelly, Dawn Titmus, Tim Harris
Designer: Mary Walsh
Design Manager: Keith Davis
Editorial Director: Lindsey Lowe
Children's Publisher: Anne O'Daly
Picture Manager: Sophie Mortimer

Picture Credits:
T=Top, C=Center, B=Bottom, L=Left, R=Right

Front Cover : All pictures Shutterstock/Thinkstock.
Inside: Alamy: Stuart Pearce 10tl; Getty Images: National Geographic 15bl; Oxyman: 26cr;
Robert Hunt Library: 26tl; Shutterstock: 11br, 18tr, 18bl, 19t, Jacqueline Abromeit 1, 22tl, Rich Carey 4, 14tl, Floridastock 5br, 18tl, Levente Gyori 11tr, Brian K. 6tl, Andrew Kerr 5tl, 19bc, Christopher Parypa 7b, Tomasz Parys 6cr, Adam Przezak 23bc, Richard Thornton 22tr; Thinkstock: Creatas 11tl, Hemera 10tr, 10bl, 23tr, iStockphoto 7tr, Photodisc 6bl, 27tr, Stockbyte 27bc; TopFoto: Granger Collection 15bl.

Brown Bear Books has made every attempt to contact the copyright holder.
If you have any information please contact licensing@brownbearbooks.co.uk

Printed in the United States of America

CONTENTS

— INTRODUCTION —

Throughout history, people have been on the move—looking for new hunting grounds, fertile land, and better climates in which to live. Ingenious inventions have led to the many modes of transportation that exist today.

Transportation is the moving of people and goods from one location to another. From bicycles, cars, trucks, and trains, to complex railroad systems, massive ocean liners, and supersonic aircraft, different means of transportation are abundant across the globe—and they differ from place to place. Have you ever wondered how the brakes in a motor vehicle work, or how an airplane lifts itself into the sky? Find out about the design and forces that make these machines operate. Here, you will also learn about the development of the railroads in the nineteenth century and surprising facts about the first "horseless carriages" (cars!) and steam locomotives.

◄ Deep-sea exploration is made possible through the use of diving suits, which enable divers to move around underwater.

◀ In many parts of the world, people use bicycle power to commute to work and to move goods and transport people.

Did you ever wonder how a supertanker carrying thousands of tons of oil stays afloat, or how a submarine or other submersible remains underwater? Find out about the technology behind these craft, as well as the aerospace design that propels rockets into space.

Subways and overland public transportation systems, such as the "L" (elevated) train in Chicago, developed out of the need for growing city populations to travel back and forth to their workplaces. In China and Japan, futuristic maglev (magnetic levitation) trains levitate off the track and speed along at up to 360 miles per hour (580 kilometers per hour) using magnets instead of wheels. But even with all these new and exciting ways to travel, the humble donkey is still one of the most common methods of transportation in the world.

▶ The steam locomotive revolutionized the way communities traded and traveled in the nineteenth century.

TRANSPORTATION

From the earliest times, people have moved from place to place in search of food and shelter, to trade goods with other people, or simply out of a sense of adventure.

Busiest railroad station: Shinjuku in Tokyo, Japan, 1.35 billion passengers every year

Busiest airport: Hartsfield-Jackson, Atlanta, Georgia, 89 million passengers every year

Busiest ferry: Star Ferry in Hong Kong, China, 26 million passengers every year

Transportation has progressed from oxen carrying loads at walking pace to supersonic jet flights and space travel. Modern modes of transportation include trains, cars, trucks, aircraft, ships, motorcycles, barges, bicycles, and spacecraft.

▲ Traveling by donkey is still a common mode of transportation for people and goods around the world.

Modern Transportation

People are always seeking ways to move themselves and their goods more quickly and easily. Fast highways, with carefully designed intersections to avoid traffic jams, now link most large cities. Some six-lane and eight-lane highways carry up to 500,000 vehicles per day. Superfast trains connect many large cities, often in different countries.

Modern transportation requires fixed installations for vehicles to travel on—railroads, roads, aircraft runways, and canals, for instance. Even at sea, in the busiest waters, shipping lanes have to be marked clearly to avoid collisions. Many stretches of road are lit at night to avoid accidents.

◀ Barges on a canal in Amsterdam, Netherlands. The city's canals were built in the seventeenth century.

The Need for Speed

Transportation has not always been so easy. It was slow and often hazardous until the nineteenth century, when the development of steam engines allowed fast railroad travel. Then, in the early twentieth century, the internal combustion engine, assembly lines, and better roads led to increased car ownership.

Modern cities now have public transportation—scheduled train, bus, and ferry services, as well as taxis. People expect shelter and comfort while they wait, so bus and train stations, airports, and ferry terminals are provided.

Freight Transportation

Freight transportation involves the movement of goods and animals by land, sea, or air. The volume

AIRFREIGHT TRANSPORTATION

There has also been an increase in freight carried by air. Air cargo can travel in special airplanes, such as the giant Russian Antonov 225, or in the holds of passenger planes. Cargoes include anything from food and books to medicines and electrical equipment.

and speed of freight carried by sea increased when the Suez Canal in Egypt was opened in 1869. This was a quicker route from Europe to Asia. Ships could pass from the Mediterranean to the Indian Ocean. Before, they had to sail around the southern tip of Africa.

The invention of container ships made it possible to move greater volumes of freight by sea. The world's busiest port, Shanghai, China, handles 567 million tons (506 million metric tonnes) of freight each year.

▲ Modern highway intersections help keep vehicles on the move.

GENERAL INFORMATION

● The Silk Road was one of the great transportation routes of ancient times. It connected China, India, and Persia (now Iran) with Europe and North Africa. Trade in silk and other fabrics, perfumes, spices, medicines, and slaves began in the time of the Chinese Han Dynasty (206 BCE–220 CE) and lasted until the late fifteenth century.

▶ A passenger aircraft takes off from a major international airport.

Q **What is a maglev train?**

A Maglev trains are the trains of the future. They have been designed without wheels and use the principle of magnetic levitation to raise them off the track. With friction almost eliminated, they can be propelled forward at speeds of up to 360 miles per hour (580 kmh). Commercial maglev train services now run in Shanghai, China, and Tobu Kyuryo, Japan. In 2011, work began on a new route in Beijing, China, and others are planned.

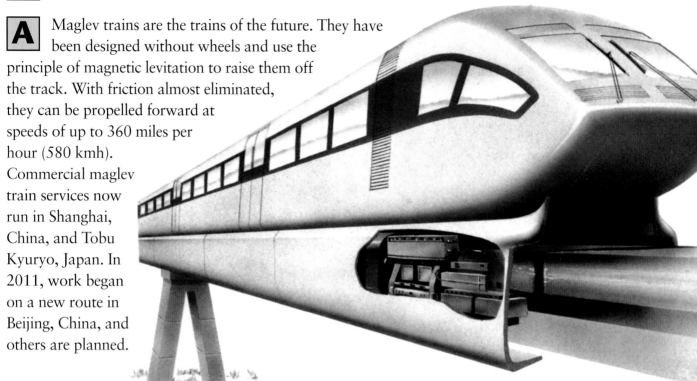

Q **How big is an oil tanker?**

A Oil tankers (right) carry crude oil and oil products. Supertankers can carry hundreds of thousands of tons of oil. The largest was over 1,500 feet (458 meters) long and 226 feet (69 m) wide. When it was fully loaded with petroleum, 82 feet (25 m) of its hull were underwater. Supertankers are difficult to steer and so heavy that they can take 3 miles (5 km) to stop completely.

Tugboats help tankers dock

Q What is a semi?

A A semi, or eighteen-wheeler (right), is a truck that consists of two separate parts. At the front is the tractor, which contains the diesel engine, the controls, the fuel tank, and the driver's cab. It has very powerful brakes. The tractor unit pulls the part called the semi-trailer, which carries the cargo.

Q Is there a "supersonic" airliner?

A "Supersonic" means faster than the speed of sound. The speed of sound is measured as 745 miles per hour (1,200 kmh) at sea level. Concorde (left) and the Tupolev Tu-144 have been the only airliners capable of flying at supersonic speed, but neither carries passengers anymore. Other commercial aircraft are not designed to fly at such speeds.

Q Who built the first steam locomotive?

A In 1804, Englishman Richard Trevithick built the first successful steam engine to run on rails. It hauled coal cars along a tram road in South Wales, United Kingdom. Trevithick later built a locomotive called *Catch Me Who Can*, which traveled at up to 10 mph (16 kmh).

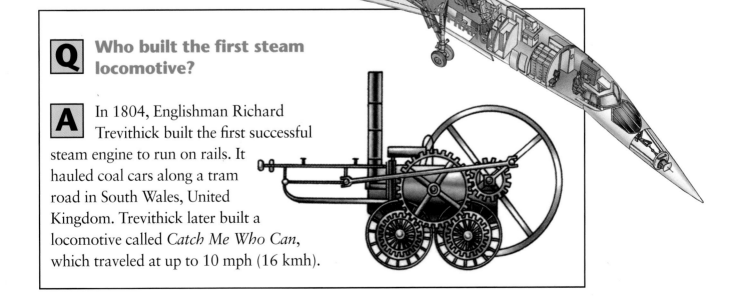

SHIPS

For thousands of years, people have used ships to trade goods, explore the world, and fight their enemies. Many modern ships and boats are used simply for pleasure.

A ship is a watertight vessel, usually powered by sails, oars, steam turbines, or internal combustion engines. Smaller craft are usually called boats, and these range from motorboats and yachts to open rowboats and racing dinghies.

The first boats were probably built around 8000 BCE. They were constructed from hollowed-out logs, bundles of reeds, and rafts made with animal skins. The ancient

▲ Modern submarines are powered by nuclear reactors.

Egyptians are known to have built boats with streamlined hulls in 3000 BCE. Around this time, sails were first used on boats in Mesopotamia. At last, human effort was not required to move a boat—as long as there was some wind.

The Age of Sail

From the thirteenth century onward, larger ships were built to carry more cargo over greater distances and explorers to distant parts of the world. Instead of one mast with a single sail, ships had numerous sails on two or three masts. Many ships had several decks built on top of each other. Passenger transportation came later: the first scheduled ship service across the Atlantic Ocean, between New York and Liverpool, England, ran in 1817.

KEY FACTS

Largest cruise ship: *Oasis of the Seas* carries 6,000 passengers and weighs 240,000 tons (225,000 t)

Largest cargo ship: TI Class supertankers Africa, Asia, Europe, and Oceania weigh 571,000 tons (518,000 t) when fully laden with oil

Fastest ship: *Spirit of Australia*, a jet-powered speedboat, reached 288 miles per hour (464 kmh) in 1978

▼ Dugout canoes, powered by people with oars, have remained largely unchanged for thousands of years.

▲ Luxurious cruise ships are like floating hotels and are popular with people who want to take a vacation on the ocean.

◀ In the nineteenth century, bigger areas of sail on multimasted clippers increased sailing speeds.

GENERAL INFORMATION

● Submarines enabled underwater travel, but they are used only by the military. Nuclear-powered submarines were built in the late twentieth century. They can stay underwater for months and do not need refueling during their twenty-five-year life span.

Steam Power

Steam power took over from sail in the later nineteenth century. It was more reliable than sail since it did not depend on winds. Other important developments followed. Strong iron hulls replaced easily damaged wood. Screw propellers replaced paddle wheels. High-speed turbine engines were developed, and diesel engines replaced steam in the early twentieth century. The age of giant cruise ships and mighty battleships had arrived.

Ships Today

Most of the world's international trade is carried on thirty-five thousand large commercial ships. These include container ships—large flat-decked craft that can be stacked high with sealed freight containers— and oil-laden supertankers that weigh up to 571,000 tons (518,000 t). Trawlers spend long periods fishing at sea. There are also countless leisure craft: cruisers, dinghies, and yachts.

UNUSUAL CRAFT

Some ships have unusual designs. Hydrofoils (right) and hovercraft are used for fast, short-range passenger services. Hydrofoils skim over the water on ski-like struts, so their hulls lift clear of the water at high speeds. Hovercraft sail on a cushion of air a few inches above the water's surface.

Q **What was the largest ship ever built?**

A The world's largest ships are cargo vessels. The largest of these are the supertankers that carry oil around the world (left). The largest one ever built was the oil tanker *Knock Nevis*. It was 1,500 feet (458 m) long and 226 feet (69 m) across. Its cavernous hull extended 82 feet (25 m) below the waterline. When full of oil, it weighed 633,000 tons (565,000 t).

Q **How does a motor lifeboat work?**

A When a distress message is received, a motor lifeboat is quickly on its way. It may be launched down a slipway or from a permanent mooring that the crew reaches by small boat. Lifeboats are designed to operate in rough seas. Most can turn themselves right side up if they capsize.

Q **What is inside a submarine?**

A A submarine (below) contains a pressurized compartment where the crew lives and works. The space between this and the outer hull contains a series of fuel, oil, water, waste, and ballast tanks. When the ballast tanks are flooded with seawater, the submarine becomes heavier than the surrounding water and sinks. When air is pumped into the tanks, forcing the water out, the submarine becomes lighter and rises.

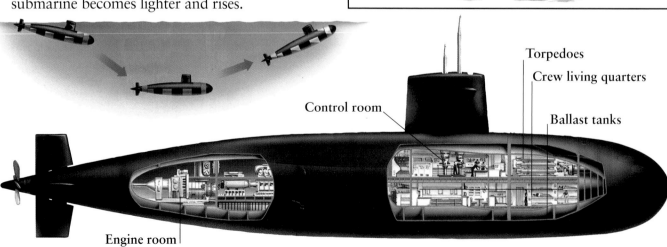

Torpedoes

Crew living quarters

Ballast tanks

Control room

Engine room

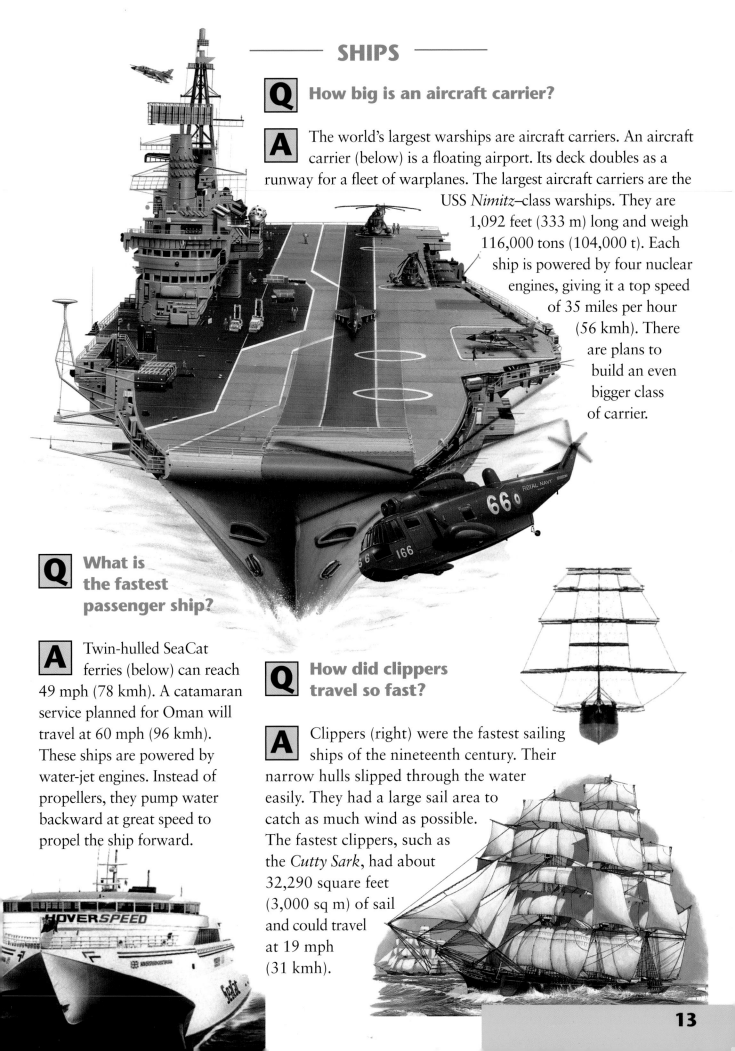

SHIPS

Q How big is an aircraft carrier?

A The world's largest warships are aircraft carriers. An aircraft carrier (below) is a floating airport. Its deck doubles as a runway for a fleet of warplanes. The largest aircraft carriers are the USS *Nimitz*–class warships. They are 1,092 feet (333 m) long and weigh 116,000 tons (104,000 t). Each ship is powered by four nuclear engines, giving it a top speed of 35 miles per hour (56 kmh). There are plans to build an even bigger class of carrier.

Q What is the fastest passenger ship?

A Twin-hulled SeaCat ferries (below) can reach 49 mph (78 kmh). A catamaran service planned for Oman will travel at 60 mph (96 kmh). These ships are powered by water-jet engines. Instead of propellers, they pump water backward at great speed to propel the ship forward.

Q How did clippers travel so fast?

A Clippers (right) were the fastest sailing ships of the nineteenth century. Their narrow hulls slipped through the water easily. They had a large sail area to catch as much wind as possible. The fastest clippers, such as the *Cutty Sark*, had about 32,290 square feet (3,000 sq m) of sail and could travel at 19 mph (31 kmh).

UNDERSEA EXPLORATION

Undersea exploration investigates the water below the ocean surface, the life it contains, and the seafloor beneath. It has given scientists a better understanding of ocean biology.

People have always wondered what lies far beneath the waves, but the ocean depths are dark and hard to explore. The British *Challenger* expedition (1872–1876) was the first major undersea survey. It searched for life by dragging the ocean bed and trawling the waters, mapped ocean temperatures and saltiness, and made depth measurements, or soundings.

The soundings provided the first strong evidence that the ocean floor was not all the same. The relatively shallow continental shelf descends steeply along continental slopes to the very deep and relatively flat abyssal plain at 14,100 feet (4,300 m). Midocean ridges rise up from this, but in places there are much deeper ocean trenches.

KEY FACTS

First major dive: William Beebe and Otis Barton in *Bathysphere* in 1930

Deepest dive: Challenger Deep, 35,814 feet (10,916 m) by Jacques Piccard in *Trieste* in 1960 and James Cameron in *Deepsea Challenger* in 2012

HYDROTHERMAL VENTS

In 1979–1980, off the coast of Ecuador in South America, scientists found cracks in the ocean floor that were spewing out super-hot water and plumes of chemicals. They called the cracks "hydrothermal vents." The water from the vents can be up to 572 degrees Fahrenheit (300 degrees Celsius). Around the cracks are animals that live nowhere else in the ocean.

The Need to Dive

To get more information, people had to dive. The pressure of the water column and the need to carry oxygen supplies meant that divers could not dive very deeply. Before the 1930s, the deepest humans could safely descend in diving suits was 100 feet (30 m). Submarines had gone deeper, but they had no windows, making them useless for seeing anything.

In 1930, the explorers William Beebe and Otis Barton dived to

▼ The different layers of the ocean and the different parts of the ocean floor.

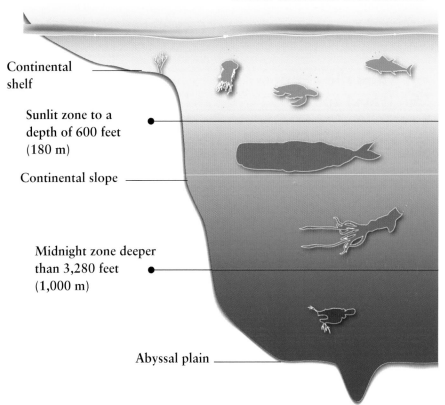

Continental shelf

Sunlit zone to a depth of 600 feet (180 m)

Continental slope

Midnight zone deeper than 3,280 feet (1,000 m)

Abyssal plain

1,427 feet (435 m) in a submersible they called the *Bathysphere*; later they took this craft down to 4,495 feet (1,370 m). They saw animals that had never been seen before.

Voyage to the Depths

The invention of sonar allowed scientists to accurately chart the depth of the ocean. Inspired by Beebe and Barton, in 1960, Jacques Piccard organized an expedition in the submersible *Trieste* to the bottom of the Marianas Trench, east of the Philippines. The deepest point *Trieste* reached (Challenger Deep) was 35,814 feet (10,916 m). James Cameron returned there in 2012 in *Deepsea Challenger*.

Crewed submersibles such as *Alvin* could be directed more easily than earlier underwater

▼ The *Bathysphere* enters the ocean near Bermuda at the start of its record-breaking dive in 1930.

craft. *Alvin* had bright spotlights to light up its surroundings and robotic arms to collect samples. *Alvin* can descend to 14,760 feet (4,500 m).

▲ The submersible *Alvin* at work.

In 1974, it explored the Great Rift Valley of the Mid-Atlantic Ridge near the Azores islands. It found evidence that new seafloor was being created along the midocean ridge. Since then, submersibles have made many exciting discoveries.

GENERAL INFORMATION

- Five nations have sent expeditions to depths greater than 11,500 feet (3,500 m). They are: the United States, France, Russia, Japan, and China.
- The submersible *Alvin* can take a crew of three down to 14,760 feet (4,500 m). Between 1964 and 2012, it made 4,400 dives.

Q How did early diving suits work?

A Early diving equipment made in the 1600s and 1700s worked by pumping air down a hose from the surface into a metal helmet over the diver's head (right). The pressure of the air inside the helmet stopped water from rising up inside.

Q How does a pressurized diving suit work?

A A pressurized diving suit (below) is supplied with air pumped from the surface through a hose. The diver can alter the air pressure inside the suit by adjusting a valve in the helmet. Heavy metal boots help to keep the diver weighted down on the seabed.

Q What is an atmospheric diving suit?

A An atmospheric diving suit (below) is a watertight suit of armor used for the deepest dives. The diver breathes air at atmospheric pressure, which is that of surface air. The heavy metal suit with watertight joints stops the huge water pressure 1,000 feet (300 m) below the surface from crushing it.

Q What is an aqualung?

A An aqualung (above) is a device that enables divers to move around freely underwater without any connection with the surface. The diver breathes air from tanks worn on the back.

Q **Why are shipwrecks explored?**

A Sunken ships can tell us a lot about the sailors who sailed them and the world they lived in. The ship's timbers may be all that is left, but sometimes the divers who explore shipwrecks (right) find tools, weapons, and some of the sailors' belongings.

Q **What animals have been found in the ocean depths?**

A Light does not reach the bottom of the ocean. Many of the fish that live there make their own light. They catch smaller fish by dangling a glowing lure over their mouth. Smaller fish swim toward the lure and straight into the fish's mouth.

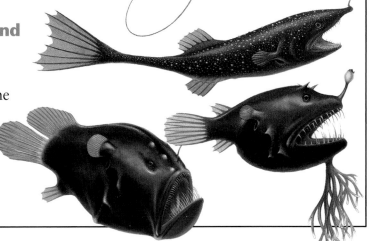

Water ballast tank

Propeller for maneuvering

Q **What was the deepest diving vessel?**

A On January 23, 1960, the submersible *Trieste* (left) descended 35,814 feet (10,916 m) into the deepest part of the Marianas Trench in the Pacific Ocean. No one has dived deeper. *Trieste*'s crew of two were protected inside a thick metal sphere beneath a large float partly filled with gasoline. When seawater flooded into the float, *Trieste* sank. To return to the surface, it dropped metal weights.

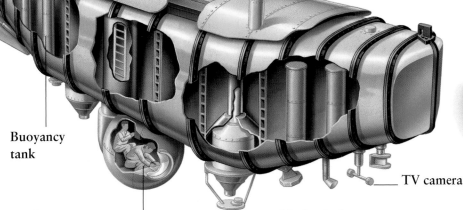

Buoyancy tank

Crew compartment

TV camera

Mechanical arm

LAND TRAVEL

People provided the earliest means of transportation, carrying goods on their backs. Horses and oxen could carry heavier loads, including people.

With the invention of the wheel and the development of carts, even bigger loads could be moved, generally following rough dirt tracks. Early civilizations such as those in Mesopotamia (in modern-day Iraq) paved their major roads to speed movement between towns. The ancient Romans developed road-building technology even further, building straight roads with only gentle slopes and drains.

KEY FACTS

Bicycles: About 1 billion worldwide

Electric bicycles: 40 million in China

Motorcycles: About 160 million worldwide

Cars: About 600 million worldwide

Trucks: More than 200 million worldwide

▼ This is Decumanus Street, in the ancient Roman city of Thamugadi, Algeria. The Romans built paved and well-drained roads so horse-drawn traffic could move quickly.

Steam Powers the Way

Until the Industrial Revolution, travel by land was generally slow. Several inventions in the eighteenth and nineteenth centuries changed the way people traveled. The first of

▲ Shinkansen trains carry 150 million passengers a year at great speed between major cities in Japan.

these was the steam engine. When used to turn wheels, running along two parallel tracks, a steam locomotive could pull much heavier loads than a team of horses ever could. The Stockton and Darlington Railway in England carried six hundred passengers at 10 miles per hour (16 kmh) on its first journey in 1825.

More powerful locomotives followed, and in the twentieth century, fast diesel- and electric-powered trains replaced steam. Modern high-speed trains pick up electric current from overhead power lines. For example, the Shinkansen trains in Japan travel at up to 200 miles per hour (320 kmh). German magnetic levitation (maglev) trains will go even faster.

Internal Combustion

The invention of the internal combustion engine in the early nineteenth century paved the way for automobile transportation toward the end of the century. Today, internal combustion engines power most cars, buses, trucks, and motorcycles. However, like the early trains, the first generation of cars was slow and unreliable. More efficient engines and smoother, straighter roads reduced journey times in the late twentieth century.

▲ A cheap method of transportation: in the back of a truck in India.

In much of the world, the car is the most popular form of transportation. Most are fueled by gasoline or diesel, though biofuels and electric cars are becoming more popular.

TWO-WHEELED TRANSPORTATION

In much of the world, bicycles (right) were the most popular mode of transportation in the twentieth century. They are relatively cheap to buy and do not require fuel. Bicycle use declined as car ownership became more common. For instance, in China, one-third of all journeys were made by bicycle in 1995—but fifteen years later, that figure had fallen to just one-fifth.

GENERAL INFORMATION

● Most major cities are linked by highways for cars and trucks. These roads have two sets of lanes, so traffic going in different directions is kept apart. Vehicles traveling at different speeds use separate lanes.

Q How are heavy loads carried by road?

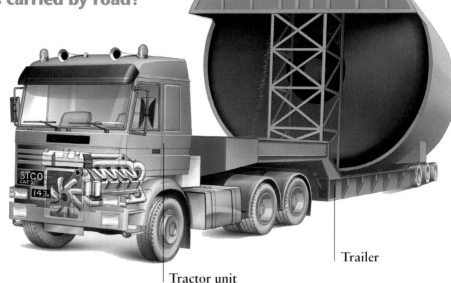

 A The largest and heaviest loads are carried on a special low, flatbed trailer pulled by a powerful tractor unit (right). This vehicle has six axles to spread the load. The tractor unit has three sets of wheels. Two of them are driven by the engine to give maximum power.

Trailer

Tractor unit

 Q How does a refrigerator truck keep its cargo cold?

Refrigeration unit

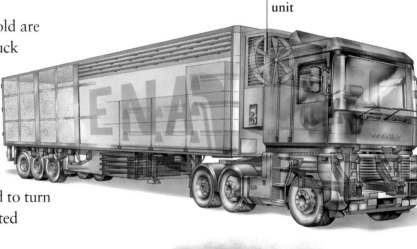

A Cargoes that have to be kept cold are transported in a refrigerator truck (right). The insulated trailer has a refrigeration unit on the front. Liquid coolant flows through pipes in the trailer and absorbs heat from the cargo. The coolant returns to the refrigeration unit and gives up its heat to the outside air. It is then compressed to turn it back into a cold liquid and recirculated through the trailer.

Q Which were the largest ever steam trains?

A The largest steam locomotives ever built were five giants called Big Boys. They were built in the 1940s for the Union Pacific Railroad. The locomotive and its coal tender (right) were almost 130 feet (40 m) long, 10 feet (3 m) wide, and 16 feet (5 m) high. Each weighed 670 tons (600 t). They pulled up to 4,480 tons (4,000 t) of freight in the Rocky Mountains.

Q **Can the sun power vehicles?**

 A Sunshine can be turned into electricity by solar cells (batteries). A vehicle covered with solar cells can produce enough electricity to drive an electric motor. A solar-powered bicycle crossed Australia at an average speed of 30 miles per hour (50 kmh). In 2011, *Sunswift Ivy* (above) set a new world speed record for a solar-powered car—55 miles per hour (89 kmh).

Q **What is the fastest train?**

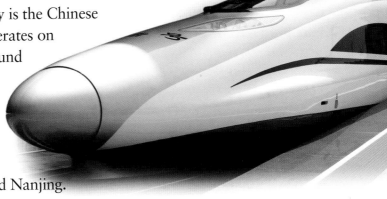

A The world's fastest train today is the Chinese CRH 380A (right), which operates on several high-speed railroad links around Shanghai. This train has a cruising speed of 217 mph (350 kmh) and a maximum operating speed of 236 mph (380 kmh), though it can go much faster. In 2010, it began to serve the route between Shanghai and Nanjing.

Q **What is a supercar?**

A Supercars are the super sedans and super sports models of the car world. They are fast, powerful, and very expensive. The Ferrari F40 (right) is a supercar. One of the world's fastest production cars, it can reach a top speed of 200 mph (325 kmh). One special feature is that the engine is behind the driver.

CARS

Cars are rubber-tired vehicles that run on roads rather than tracks. Most are powered by internal combustion engines with gasoline or diesel fuel.

A Frenchman, Nicolas Cugnot, built the first self-powered road vehicle in 1769. It was a three-wheeled steam engine designed to pull cannons, but it was never used. Modern car design began to take shape in the late nineteenth century. German engineers Gottlieb Daimler and Karl Benz both created engine-driven cars in 1886. A few years later, Frenchman Emile Levassor built a car with spring suspension (for a smoother ride) and gears.

▲ The Model T Ford was the first mass production car. Its top speed was 45 mph (72 kmh).

Car Engines

The heart of a car is its internal combustion engine. Gasoline or diesel and air are ignited in a combustion chamber, and hot, expanding gas pushes pistons. The motion of the pistons turns the car's axles, and these turn its wheels.

A transmission system (gearbox) uses gears to match the engine's speed to the desired road speed. The clutch, which may be automatic or manual (stick shift), controls the transmission. Oil protects the various engine

KEY FACTS

First production car: Benz Velo; 134 were built in 1895

Most popular car: 21.5 million Volkswagen Beetles built 1938–2003

Fastest production car: Bugatti Veyron 16.4 Super Sport, 268 mph (431 kmh)

Most fuel-efficient production car: Volkswagen XL1, 261 miles (420 km) to the gallon (3.8 liters) of diesel

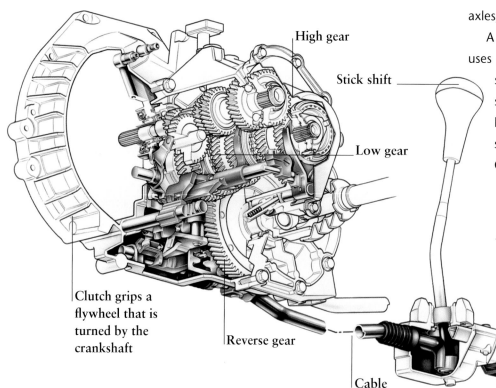

High gear

Stick shift

Low gear

Clutch grips a flywheel that is turned by the crankshaft

Reverse gear

Cable

◀ A manual transmission (gearbox) of a car. The diagram shows the clutch, the different gear wheels, and the stick shift, which the driver operates to change gear.

SOME FEATURES OF A MODERN CAR

Modern cars have comfortable seats and safety features such as airbags. Car manufacturers devote huge amounts of money to improved style and greater engine efficiency. Many cars now have computers to control in-car temperature and humidity, GPS (Global Positioning System) satellite navigation (right) to direct drivers to specified locations, and high-quality sound systems for music players and radios.

parts from rubbing against each other, and a cooling system keeps the engine from overheating. The exhaust removes waste gases. The suspension is a set of springs and shock absorbers that soften unevenness on the road and help the vehicle take corners easily.

Mass Production

American Henry Ford (1863–1947) began a revolution in car manufacturing. He developed the assembly line that made mass production possible around 1913. Cars that were being assembled moved slowly along a conveyor belt. Each worker had a few simple tasks to perform on each car, over and over, many times each day. Many more cars could be produced in a day, and so Ford could sell them more cheaply than other car models. By 1927, fifteen million of Ford's Model Ts had rolled off the production line.

More Efficient Cars

By the 1960s, the huge increase in car use was causing pollution problems. Manufacturers began to make cars smaller and more efficient. To reduce our reliance on oil, biofuels (made from vegetable oils, for instance) are now used instead in some cars. Also, battery-powered cars have been developed to protect Earth's resources.

▶ An electric car has its battery recharged by the roadside in Oslo, Norway.

GENERAL INFORMATION

- Car ownership varies greatly from nation to nation. In the United States, there are more than eight hundred cars for every thousand people, and in Japan, the figure is six hundred. In Bangladesh, however, there are only two cars per thousand people.

Q How is a modern car built for safety?

A A modern car has complex machinery and structures built into the bodywork (right) so that it is safe. A strong body frame is designed to protect the occupants in a crash. An antilock braking system (ABS) enables the car to brake without skidding by releasing and reapplying the brakes many times every second. The steering column is made in sections that will collapse in the event of a crash.

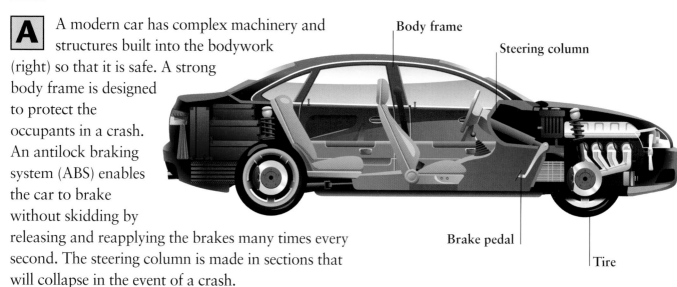

Body frame

Steering column

Brake pedal

Tire

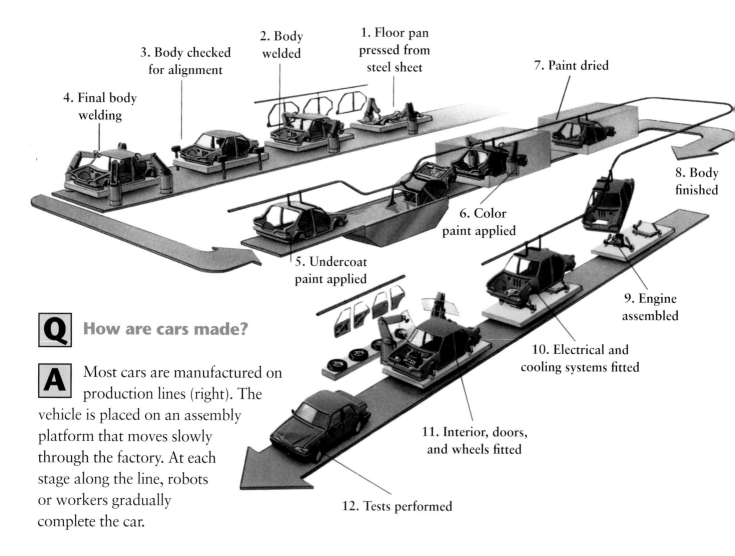

3. Body checked for alignment

2. Body welded

1. Floor pan pressed from steel sheet

7. Paint dried

4. Final body welding

8. Body finished

6. Color paint applied

5. Undercoat paint applied

9. Engine assembled

10. Electrical and cooling systems fitted

11. Interior, doors, and wheels fitted

12. Tests performed

Q How are cars made?

A Most cars are manufactured on production lines (right). The vehicle is placed on an assembly platform that moves slowly through the factory. At each stage along the line, robots or workers gradually complete the car.

Q Why do car engines need oil?

A As a car travels, many of its parts move against each other. The different parts of the engine (right) move at high speed. Oil is pumped from the sump to lubricate the bearings, pistons, and other components, allowing the metal parts to move without causing wear or generating heat through friction. Some vehicles use special oils to allow them to be driven in very cold conditions.

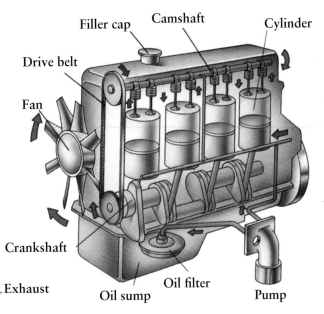

Filler cap Camshaft Cylinder
Drive belt
Fan
Crankshaft
Exhaust
Oil sump Oil filter Pump

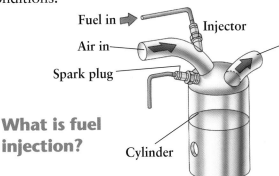

Fuel in
Air in
Spark plug
Injector
Cylinder

Q What is fuel injection?

A Car engines burn fuel in closed cylinders. A fuel injection system pumps a precise amount of fuel into the cylinders as air is sucked in (above). The mixture is then ignited by a spark plug, and the waste gases flow through the exhaust.

Q What did the first cars look like?

A The first cars were built in the 1880s. To begin with, engines were built into carriages normally pulled by horses. These "horseless carriages" had simple controls.

Q How are race cars designed to go fast?

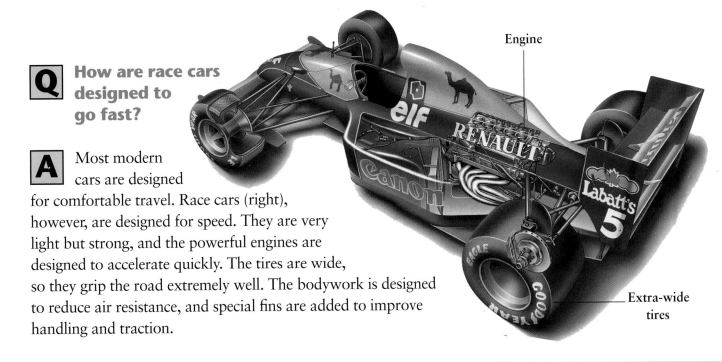

Engine

Extra-wide tires

A Most modern cars are designed for comfortable travel. Race cars (right), however, are designed for speed. They are very light but strong, and the powerful engines are designed to accelerate quickly. The tires are wide, so they grip the road extremely well. The bodywork is designed to reduce air resistance, and special fins are added to improve handling and traction.

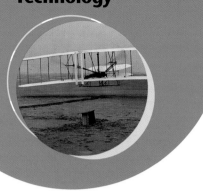

FLIGHT

Even before the ancient Greek myth of Icarus—who flew on wings of wax and feathers—people have wanted to fly. That wish has become reality only in the last two hundred years or so.

KEY FACTS

Passenger aircraft cruising height: About 39,370 feet (12,000 m)

Passenger aircraft cruising speed: Around 560 mph (900 kmh)

Biggest passenger aircraft: Airbus A380 seats up to 850 passengers on two decks

Fastest aircraft: Lockheed SR-71 "Blackbird," 2,193 mph (3,530 kmh) in 1976

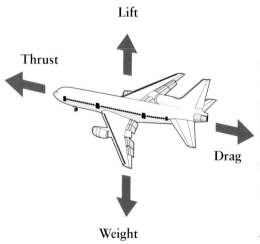

Three forces act on an aircraft when it is airborne. Since a plane is heavier than air, it can fly only if air flows over its wings fast enough to produce an upward force called lift. This force has to be stronger than the force of gravity if the plane is to stay in the air. A third force—thrust—is produced by the aircraft's engines and drives the plane forward. Thrust must be stronger than drag, the resistance of the air, for the plane to fly.

◀ The four different forces that act on a plane as it is flying.

▲ Modern jet aircraft carry hundreds of passengers, for thousands of miles, without refueling.

Early Flight

The earliest form of air transportation was by hot-air balloon. The first manned flight took the pilot about 5 miles (8 km) near Paris in 1783. However, this was a slow and unreliable means of transportation, being completely dependent on the wind.

Pioneers such as George Cayley (1773–1857) and Otto Lilienthal (1848–1896) experimented with

▶ Not all flight is powered. Hang gliders make the most of breezes to stay airborne.

engineless gliders. However, controlled, powered flight was mastered only in 1903 when an internal combustion engine and reliable propellers allowed Orville and Wilbur Wright to fly 118 feet (36 m). Improvements followed, and the commercial flights began after World War I (1914–1918).

Jet Engines

Until the outbreak of World War II in 1939, planes had engines that drove propellers. These converted engine power into thrust. Ideas for a jet engine, which could increase flying speeds, emerged independently in England and Germany in the 1930s. Fans inside a jet engine suck air through them. As the air is forced out of the back of the jet engine, it pushes the aircraft forward.

The German He 178 was the first jet plane and made its maiden flight in 1939. The need for faster warplanes during World War II accelerated the development of jet technology, and better planes followed. After the war, jet engines were used increasingly to power passenger aircraft, from the de Havilland Comet in 1952 to the world's first supersonic passenger plane, Concorde. Concorde flew between London, New York, and Paris between 1976 and 2003, cruising at 1,330 miles per hour (2,140 kmh). Even faster planes have been built for military use.

HELICOPTER FLIGHT

The first operational helicopter flew in 1936. Full-scale production started in the United States three years later. The thrust and lift in a helicopter is provided by engine-driven rotor blades above the craft. Although they were first used for military roles, helicopters now also carry passengers and deliver food aid in emergency relief operations.

GENERAL INFORMATION

● The longest ever flight was made in a propeller-driven Cessna plane. Americans Robert Timm and John Cook kept it airborne for sixty-five days in 1957–1958. The Cessna was refueled in flight.

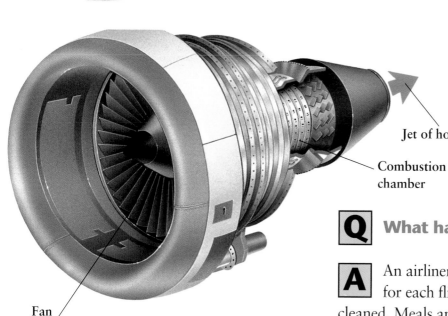

Q How does an airplane stay in the air?

A Airplanes (left) can fly because of the shape of their wings. The top of the wing is more curved than the bottom. Air rushing over the top of the wings travels farther and faster than the air flowing underneath. This produces lower air pressure above the wings than below them (below), causing the wings to lift.

Airflow

Jet of hot air

Combustion chamber

Fan

Q What happens before takeoff?

A An airliner (below) is carefully prepared for each flight. The passenger cabin is cleaned. Meals and luggage are loaded. The fuel tanks are filled. Engineers check the plane, and the crew makes its preflight checks.

Q How does a jet engine work?

A A large spinning fan at the front of the engine (above) sucks in air. The air is then compressed and heated by burning fuel in the combustion chamber. This makes the air expand quickly. A jet of hot air rushes out of the back of the engine and pushes the airplane forward.

Q What did the first airplane look like?

A The first airplane, called *Flyer 1* (right), flew in 1903. It was made from wood. It had two wings covered with fabric, one above the other, and the pilot lay down on the lower wing to fly it.

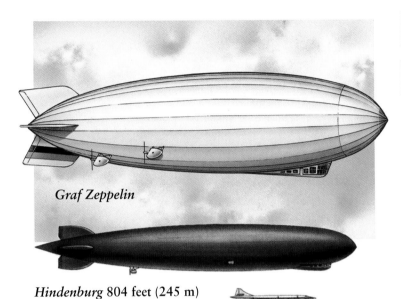

Graf Zeppelin

Hindenburg 804 feet (245 m)

Concorde 202.4 feet (61.6 m)

Q What is a Zeppelin?

A A Zeppelin (left) is a giant airship named after its inventor, Count Ferdinand von Zeppelin. The Zeppelins were built in Germany between 1900 and the 1930s. The biggest passenger-carrying Zeppelins were the *Graf Zeppelin* and the *Hindenburg*. They carried passengers across the Atlantic Ocean. Zeppelins could fly without wings because they were filled with hydrogen gas. This is lighter than air and made the airships float upward.

Q How does a glider work?

A Gliders are aircraft that fly without any engines. Instead, they rely on air currents to remain in the air. Gliders are built of light materials and usually have very large wings in proportion to their body size. This enables them to gain the maximum lift from the currents. If a glider pilot finds currents of rising air—called thermals and often located under clouds—the aircraft can stay aloft for hours at a time.

GLOSSARY

ABS (antilock braking system) A system of brakes that stops a vehicle's wheels from locking and prevents skidding on the road.

abyssal plain An underwater plain, or flat area, of the ocean floor that is between 10,000 and 20,000 feet (3,000 and 6,000 m) deep.

biofuels A fuel that is made from living matter—for example, corn, sugarcane, or vegetable oil.

clipper ship A fast sailing ship with masts and a concave (curved inward) bow (front end) used widely in the nineteenth century.

fuel injection The pumping of fuel under pressure into a combustion chamber in an internal combustion engine.

GPS Global Positioning System is a method of navigation that uses satellites to accurately track a vehicle's movement and guide the driver to a destination. Newer vehicles have built-in GPS, also sometimes called "satnav."

internal combustion engine An engine that burns gasoline, oil, or other fuel with air inside the engine to produce hot gases that generate motion to make a vehicle run.

jet engine An engine used in aircraft that uses jet propulsion to create forward thrust.

mass production A way of making large numbers of one item using an automated mechanical process on a production line.

public transportation Trains, buses, and subways for the public to use, which run on set routes and charge set fares.

Roman road A straight, paved road built by the Romans all across the ancient Roman Empire. Some Roman roads in Europe are still in use today.

solar cell A battery that converts the sun's radiation into electricity.

sonar A system that sends out sound pulses and measures their return distance to gauge the ocean's depth and find objects underwater, such as shipwrecks.

steam engine An engine that uses steam to generate motion, such as steam locomotives in the nineteenth century.

submersible A craft designed to travel underwater, such as a submarine or bathysphere.

supersonic Something that travels at a speed greater than the speed of sound. Concorde aircraft were supersonic.

transmission The mechanism by which power is passed from the engine to the wheels of a motor vehicle. In the US, most vehicles have an automatic transmission.

turbine engine An engine that produces power from a wheel revolving from a fast-moving flow of water, steam, or air, etc.

FURTHER READING

Books

Buckley, James Jr. *Who Were the Wright Brothers?* New York: Grosset & Dunlap, 2014.

DK editors. *Transportation: DK Eyewitness Books*. New York: DK Children's, 2012.

Solomon, Brian. *North American Railroad Family Trees: An Infographic History*. Minneapolis, MN: Voyageur Press, 2013.

Spengler, Kremena T. *An Illustrated Timeline of Transportation*. Visual Timelines in History. Chicago: Picture Window Books, 2011.

Umstot, Mary. *How Boats Work*. Seattle: CreateSpace Independent Publishing, 2014.

Websites

America on the Move: Smithsonian
amhistory.si.edu/onthemove/exhibition/
Learn about the fascinating history of transportation in the US. With stories and photos about river routes, canals, and shipping, the early railroad, and how cars and airplanes changed the way people live.

National Maritime Historical Society
www.seahistory.org/
Discover famous ships and vessels that made a "splash" in American history, including Great Lakes ghost ship the *Cornelia B. Windiate*, the *Arabia* steamboat—buried under a Kansas cornfield for 150 years, the USS *Constitution*, and more.

What Is Aeronautics? NASA
www.grc.nasa.gov/WWW/k-12/UEET/
StudentSite/aeronautics.html
Here, NASA offers a guide to aeronautics, including the dynamics and history of flight, all about airplanes and their engines, and aeronautics games. Also includes tips on studying for a career in aerospace.

INDEX